ONE DIRECTION

STRAIGHT TO THE TOP

By Riley Brooks

■SCHOLASTIC

Straight to the Top photo credits:

Front cover: © Ian West/AP; back cover: © John Marshall /AP

p. 1: © Rex Features/Associated Press; p. 3: © Rex Features/Associated Press; p. 6: © Ian West/Associated Press; p. 7: © Ian West/Associated Press; p. 8: © Anthony Devlin/Associated Press; p. 10: © Charles Sykes/Associated Press; p. 11: © Owen Sweeney/Rex Features/Associated Press; p. 12: © Anthony Devlin/Associated Press; p. 14: © Charles Sykes/ Associated Press; p. 15: © Ian West/Associated Press; p. 16: © Stewart Cook/Rex Features/Associated Press; p. 18: © Owen Sweeney/Rex Features/Associated Press; p. 19: © Charles Sykes/Associated Press; p. 20: © Charles Sykes/ Associated Press; p. 22: © Charles Sykes/Associated Press; p. 23: © Charles Sykes/Associated Press; p. 24: © Charles Sykes/Associated Press; p. 26: © Arthur Mola/Associated Press; p. 27: © Charles Sykes/Associated Press; p. 28: © Dominic Lipinski/Associated Press; p. 31: © Ian West/Associated Press; p. 32: © Yui Mok/Associated Press; p. 33: © David Rowland/Rex Features/Associated Press; p. 34: © AGF s.r.l./Rex Features/Associated Press; p. 36: © Frank Micelotta/Associated Press; p. 37: © John Marshall/Associated Press; p. 38: © Charles Sykes/Associated Press; p. 40: © David Rowland/Rex Features/Associated Press; p. 41: © Nikki To/Rex Features/Associated Press; p. 42: © Yui Mok/Associated Press; p. 44: © Charles Sykes/Associated Press; p. 45: © Ian West/Associated Press; p. 46: © Frank Micelotta/Associated Press; p. 48: © Chris Pizzello/Associated Press; p. 49: © David Rowland/Rex Features/ Associated Press; p. 50: © IBL/Rex Features/Associated Press

Quiz Book photo credits

Interior: Page 52: © Yul Mok/Associated Press; Page 53: © Steve Parsons/Associated Press; Pages 54-55: © Dominic Lipinski/Associated Press; Page 57: © Getty Images; Page 61: © IBL/Rex Features/Associated Press; Page 65: © IBL/Rex Features/Associated Press; Page 67: © Newspix via Getty Images; Page 68: © NBCU Photo Bank via Getty Images; Page 69: © Nikki To/Rex Features/Associated Press; Page 71: © IBL/Rex Features/Associated Press; Page 73: © WireImage/ Getty Images; Page 74: © John Marshall/Associated Press; Page 75: © Getty Images; Page 78: © IBL/Rex Features/ Associated Press; Page 79: © Charles Sykes /Associated Press; Page 81: © IBL/Rex Features/Associated Press; Page 83: © Dominic Lipinski/Associated Press; Page 84: © Yui Mok/Associated Press; Page 85: © Film Magic/Getty Images; Page 86: © Getty Images; Page 89: © Film Magic/Getty Images; Page 91: © Credit Barket/PictureGroup via AP Images; Page 93: © WireImage/Getty Images; Page 95: © WireImage/Getty Images

Vector graphic of fans: © Sabri Deniz Kizil/Shutterstock

Sticker sheet: pink hearts: © MarketOlya/Shutterstock; stars: © beboy/Shutterstock; guitars: © Monkik/Shutterstock; peace sign: © vectomart/Shutterstock; microphone: © DVARG/Shutterstock; shooting yellow star: © Oculo/Shutterstock; music notes: © zphoto/Shutterstock.

This book was first published in the US in 2012 by Scholastic Inc as
One Direction: Straight to the Top!
and *One Direction: Quiz Book.*

Scholastic Children's Books,
Euston House, 24 Eversholt Street,
London NW1 1DB, UK

A division of Scholastic Ltd
London ~ New York ~ Toronto ~ Sydney ~ Auckland
Mexico City ~ New Delhi ~ Hong Kong

Published in the UK by Scholastic Ltd, 2012

ISBN 978 1407 13736 0

Printed and bound in the UK by Bell and Bain

20 19 18 17 16 15 14 13

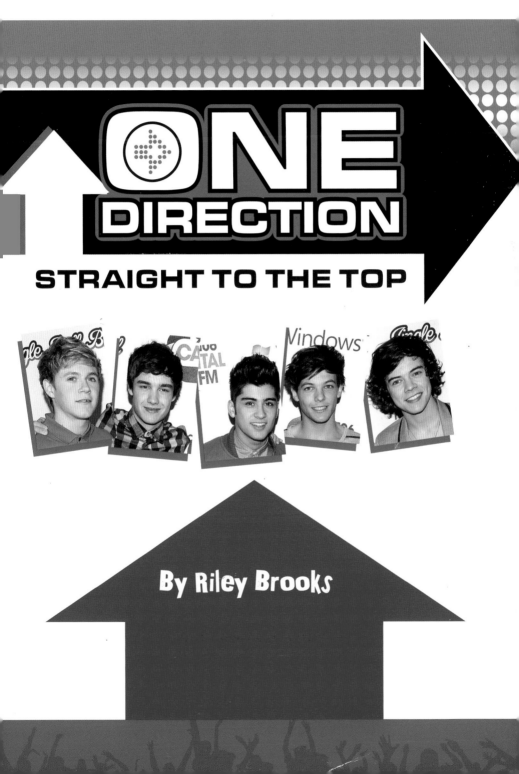

ONE DIRECTION

STRAIGHT TO THE TOP

By Riley Brooks

Table of Contents

Table of Contents

Introduction

The first time One Direction appeared together on stage, they were five very nervous boys who barely knew each other. They were performing on *The X Factor* and were worried they were going to be sent home. But these days the guys of 1D – Niall, Zayn, Liam, Harry, and Louis – are as close as brothers!

Now One Direction is taking the music world by storm with a number one album, sold-out concerts, and plenty of adoring fans. Despite their new-found fame, boys will be boys, and the boys of One Direction are every bit as fun and down-to-earth as their fans imagine them to be!

CHAPTER 1

Niall Horan

Adorable blond Niall James Horan was born on 13th September, 1993, in Ireland. His parents, Maura and Bobby, split up when Niall was five, but they have both always been very supportive of his dreams.

Niall's dad and aunt knew they had a star on their hands when one day they heard him singing in the car and thought the radio was on! "Exactly the same thing happened to Michael Bublé with his dad," Niall explained to digitalspy.com. "He's my absolute hero so I like the fact we have a similar story." Niall's family was very proud of his talent. They got him a guitar for Christmas and he has been playing ever since.

Niall's talent set him apart from the other students at his school, Coláiste Mhuire. In fact, Niall sang in a few local concerts while he was in school. All of those performances helped Niall prepare for his *X Factor* audition, but he was still pretty nervous on the big day! He stood in line with over 10,000 other hopefuls to sing for just a few minutes. Luckily, Niall made a big impression and was invited to continue with the competition.

Full Name: Niall James Horan

Nickname: **Kyle**

Birthday: **13ᵗʰ September, 1993**

Siblings: **older brother, Greg**

Home Town: **Mullingar, Ireland**

Favourite Film: *Grease*

Favourite Bands: **The Script, Ed Sheeran, Bon Jovi**

Dislikes: **mayonnaise**

Twitter Handle: **@NiallOfficial**

Star Stats

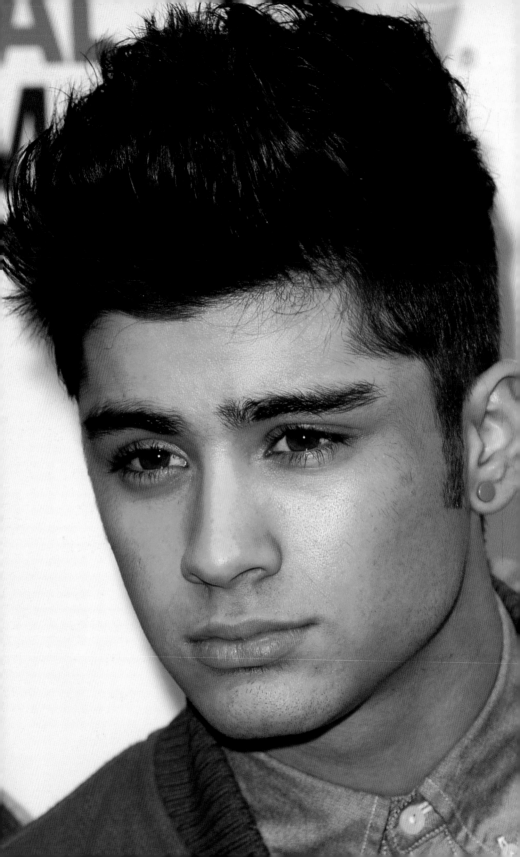

CHAPTER 2

Zayn Malik

Z ain Javadd Malik, better known as Zayn, was born on 12th January, 1993. Zayn gets his charm from his father, Yaser, and his energy from his mother, Tricia. "I was a bit of a handful when I was a kid because I was quite hyperactive …" Zayn told thesun.co.uk. Zayn has always been proof that good things come in small packages – Zayn was one of the shortest kids in his year, but his big personality more than made up for it!

Along with his three younger sisters, Doniya, Waliyha, and Safaa, Zayn grew up near Bradford in England. Things weren't always easy for Zayn. He and his sisters were often bullied because of their mixed heritage, and they had to change schools several times.

Things got better for Zayn when he began school at Tong High School, where he took up drama. As soon as Zayn got up on stage, he was completely comfortable in the spotlight. Steve Gates, a teacher at Tong High, told thetelegraphandargus.co.uk, "Zayn is a model student who excelled in all the performing arts subjects … He was always a star performer in all the school productions." So, it was really no surprise to anyone when Zayn decided to audition for *The X Factor* – his friends and family already knew he was a star!

Star Stats

Full Name: Zain Javadd Malik

Nickname: Wayne, Zayn
Birthday: 12th January, 1993
Siblings: younger sisters, Doniya, Waliyha, and Safaa
Home Town: Bradford, England
Favourite Film: *Scarface*
Favourite Bands: Usher, Robin Thicke, Michael Jackson, Ne-Yo
Bad Habit: checking himself in every mirror he sees
Twitter Handle: @zaynmalik

CHAPTER 3

Liam Payne

Liam James Payne gave his parents, Karen and Geoff, quite a scare when he was born on 29th August, 1993, in Wolverhampton, England. Little Liam had health problems from the moment he took his first breath. He told sugarscape.com, "They discovered that one of my kidneys wasn't working properly and it had scarred … I have to be careful not to drink too much, even water, and I have to keep myself as healthy as possible." Luckily, Liam's parents and older sisters, Ruth and Nicola, always took great care of him!

In high school, Liam was one of the stars on the cross-country team. He also took boxing lessons.

When Liam wasn't playing sports, he focused on music. Liam studied music technology at the City of Wolverhampton College. He had considered a job behind the scenes in the music business, but Liam always secretly dreamed of being a singer. He had actually auditioned for *The X Factor* back in 2008, but didn't make it very far. Simon Cowell encouraged him to come back in two years – and it's a good thing he did, since the second time around landed Liam in One Direction!

CHAPTER 4

Harry Styles

Harry Edward Styles was born on 1st February, 1994, in Evesham, England. His parents, Anne and Des, knew early on that they had a star on their hands – Harry always loved singing, especially Elvis Presley's songs. Harry's parents got a divorce when he was seven, but he and his older sister, Gemma, always got to spend plenty of time with both parents growing up.

As Harry got older, his love of music really took centre stage. While attending Holmes Chapel Comprehensive School, Harry became the lead singer for the band White Eskimo with friends Haydn Morris, Nick Clough, and Will Sweeny. Harry's bubbly personality made him the perfect front man for the band. They performed at school events, Battle of the Bands, and even at a wedding! Then, Harry decided to audition for *The X Factor*. He initially entered as a solo performer. He sang "Isn't She Lovely" by Stevie Wonder and really had fun with it. But Harry had to leave his bandmates behind when he made it through the first auditions. Luckily, Harry's White Eskimo friends have been really supportive and are big One Direction fans.

Johanna and Mark Tomlinson got a fantastic early Christmas present when Louis William Tomlinson was born on 24th December, 1991, in Doncaster, England. Soon the Tomlinson family grew to include younger sisters Charlotte, Félicité, and twins Daisy and Phoebe. When their parents split up in 2002, Louis really stepped up to take the best care of his sisters possible.

It was clear that the Tomlinson kids all had talent at a very young age. Daisy and Phoebe started acting as babies on the popular TV programme *Fat Friends*. Louis was an extra on the same programme, had a role in the feature-length drama *If I Had You*, and appeared on the award-winning television series *Waterloo*

Road. Louis loved being in front of the camera, but music was always his biggest passion.

For high school, Louis attended Hall Cross School, where he starred in the school's musicals and plays. Since Louis had always loved being in the spotlight, it was no surprise to any of his classmates that he auditioned for *The X Factor* and joined One Direction. Everyone was really proud of Louis for achieving his dreams and they are all cheering him on from back home.

Star Stats

Full Name: Louis William Tomlinson

Nickname: Hughy

Birthday: 24th December, 1991

Siblings: younger sisters, Charlotte, Félicité, Daisy, and Phoebe

Home Town: Doncaster, England

Favourite Film: *Grease*

Favourite Bands: The Fray, Bombay Bicycle Club

Best Friend: Harry Styles

Twitter Handle: @Louis_Tomlinson

CHAPTER 6

X Marks the Spot

*T*he *X Factor* is one of the hottest shows in Britain. (In fact, it's such a hit, they've made a version for the US too!) Fans tune in every series to watch hopefuls audition to compete for a recording contract. Contestants can enter in one of four categories – boys, girls, over-twenty-five-year-olds, or groups.

After several rounds of open auditions, selected contestants go through to boot camp and mentoring before one final audition. The remaining contestants then compete on live TV each week for viewers' votes. Getting past the first round of auditions is a big deal, but getting to the live finals is a dream come true for any singer – and the boys of One Direction are no exception.

Liam, Harry, Niall, Louis, and Zayn each auditioned in their home towns for the chance to compete on 2010's series seven in the boys category. Each of the guys picked songs to show off their unique styles. All five of the guys made it to the boot-camp round, but then they ran into trouble. Zayn had an especially difficult time with the dancing. Unfortunately, none of the guys made it through the boot-camp round.

That would have been the end of the story if the judges hadn't had a brilliant idea. They suggested that Liam, Harry, Niall, Louis, and Zayn form a boy band and continue through the competition as a group. It was an interesting proposal, as Zayn explained to teenvogue.com: "Before we got together as a band we were kind of each other's competition because we're from the same category [on *X Factor*]. But as soon as we got put together we all got on really well. We all went to Harry's place and stayed there together to get to know each other."

The boys only had a short time to get their new act together, and an even shorter time to come up with a name for their group. Harry suggested *One Direction* since all of the boys had the same goal, and, with that, the band was born!

The rest of the competition was tough, but the guys did a great job. They made it all the way to the final round singing songs like "My Life Would Suck Without You", "Kids in America", and "Chasing Cars". Sadly, One Direction didn't win. They finished in third place. Fans were disappointed, but they cheered up when "Forever Young", a single One Direction had recorded in case they won, was leaked on the Internet!

Usually, only the winner of *The X Factor* gets a recording contract, but one of the programme's judges, Simon Cowell, offered One Direction a contract with his own record label, Syco Records. After a four-month *X Factor* tour, One Direction went straight into the recording studio to create their first album.

CHAPTER 7

Up All Night

Recording an album was a totally new experience for One Direction, but it was a challenge they were ready for! "Thankfully, we got lots of say in the album, actually," Liam told irishtimes.com. "We got to choose a lot of the songs and that sort of stuff ..." The guys even helped write some of the songs they recorded! Zayn told irishtimes.com, "When you write your own music … it can be quite hard to express it to people. But we always felt comfortable. And we had each other to show our ideas to."

One Direction's first single, "What Makes You Beautiful," was released on 11th September, 2011, in the UK and immediately shot to number one in the Singles Chart. "Gotta Be You," the guys' second single was released on 13th November, 2011, and their debut album, *Up All Night*, hit the shelves a week later on 21st November, 2011. The album rocketed to number two in the UK charts and quickly reached the top ten in eighteen other countries.

One Direction promoted their album with appearances on TV programmes, radio stations, and at award shows. The guys won

the 2011 4Music Awards for "Best Group", "Best Breakthrough", and "Best Video", and beat Adele to win the 2012 Brit Award for "Best British Single" for "What Makes You Beautiful" – a really high achievement. They also went on tour all over the UK, with most shows selling out within minutes. It was official: One Direction was a pop sensation.

CHAPTER 8

The New British Invasion

One Direction wasn't just content with being the UK's favourite boy band – they wanted to conquer the whole world! One Direction made history on 13th March, 2012, when they released *Up All Night* at number one on the American charts. They were the first British group to ever have a number one debut in the US. "We simply cannot believe that we are number one in America," Harry told cbsnews.com. "It's beyond a dream come true for us."

Liam, Zayn, Niall, Harry, and Louis spent a lot of time in America promoting their album. They made appearances to meet their US fans and sign autographs, opened for American boy band Big Time Rush on a leg of their sold-out "Better With U" Tour, and made guest appearances on several TV shows including Nickelodeon's *iCarly* and *The Today Show* on 12th March, 2012. Over 10,000 fans came out to see them perform that morning on *The Today Show*. "It was incredible," Liam told hitflix.com. "When we came to the front of the stage and saw how many people there were, it was literally my most amazing moment so far." One Direction even performed as the musical guest on the 7th April, 2011, episode of

Saturday Night Live, the guys' favourite comedy show!

With their singles and album racing up the US charts, One Direction announced a summer US tour, which sold out in record time. The guys also performed "What Makes You Beautiful" at the 2012 *Nickelodeon Kids' Choice Awards.* The performance was definitely one of the favourites of the night. The guys are also in discussions with Nickelodeon to develop a show. How cool would that be?

US fans can't seem to get enough of One Direction, and it's clear that the British invasion won't be stopping any time soon!

CHAPTER 9

Backstage Pass

The guys of One Direction spend a LOT of time together, so it's a good thing that they get along so well. Since the guys can't take their families and friends on tour with them, they've become like family to each other. Louis and Harry even rented a flat together in North London!

When they aren't touring or working, the guys try to catch up with their families and friends as much as they can! "[Our mums] all got the same sort of mum thing where they're all really upset when ... we leave home, but at the same time they know we're going out and enjoying what we do. But they miss us," Liam told teenvogue.com. The boys check in with lots of phone calls and emails, but nothing is as good as a visit home! "[O]bviously it's a great experience for us, but also we also make our mums proud. We've found friends in each other, but also our parents are friends," Louis explained to teenvogue.com.

One Direction spends a lot of time on the road these days, but the guys know how to make their work fun. They have a blast messing around in their hotels, shooting funny videos to post for their fans, playing pranks on one another, listening to music, watching

films, and ordering room service!

Of course, the guys try to check out cool places in every city they visit. They love to go out to eat and see the sites and take a break from work. So don't be surprised if you see Zayn, Niall, Harry, Liam, or Louis out and about in your town if they have a concert nearby!

CHAPTER 10

Fab Future

One Direction's career is just getting warmed up. With a number one album, chart-topping singles, and tour dates, the guys are very busy. But, luckily for One Direction's fans, Liam, Harry, Zayn, Louis, and Niall aren't slowing down any time soon!

The group plans to record their next album by the end of 2012. Niall told *The National Post*, "In the summer, we're going to get back and start a new record. We want to bring out a record nearly every year/every year and a half." The guys have already started working on new songs and are meeting with producers. "I think we'd like to do more writing on the next album," Liam told hitflix.com. Writing great new songs and recording music that their fans will love is always going to be the band's number one priority.

As important as their music is, One Direction has lots of other opportunities coming their way, too. They have a development deal in place with Nickelodeon for a TV programme and have signed on to partner with some cool brands like Pokémon and Nokia. The guys would love to possibly work on a clothing line, make some film appearances, and headline

a global tour! "The ultimate goal would be to do a big, worldwide tour. That would be the most amazing thing we could do," Liam told suntimes.com. So keep your eyes peeled for a 1D show near you soon!

One thing is certain, no matter what the future holds, it's looking very bright for the cuties of One Direction!

1D Online

Want more info on One Direction?
<u>Check out their official sites:</u>

Official Website: www.onedirectionmusic.com

Official Twitter: @onedirection

ONE DIRECTION

QUIZ BOOK

By Riley Brooks

The 1D Story

One Direction got their start on the seventh series of the TV singing competition *The X Factor*. Fans tune in every series to vote as singers compete in four different categories to win a record deal. The categories are boys, girls, over 25-year-olds, and groups.

Liam Payne, Harry Styles, Niall Horan, Louis Tomlinson, and Zayn Malik each had incredible auditions in the boys' category. Niall sang "So Sick", Zayn sang "Let Me Love You", Liam sang "Cry Me a River", Harry sang "Isn't She Lovely", and Louis sang "Hey There Delilah". All five of the guys advanced through several rounds all the way to boot camp, but they were each cut at this round.

Luckily, the story doesn't end there! The judges, including music mogul Simon Cowell, had the brilliant idea that Liam, Harry, Niall, Louis, and Zayn continue through the competition as a boy band. Harry suggested the name *One Direction* for their new group, as they all had the same goal, and, with that, One Direction was born.

1D made it all the way to the final round singing songs like "My Life Would Suck Without You", "Kids in America", and "Chasing Cars". Sadly, One Direction finished in third place, and Matt Cardle took first place. But Simon Cowell was so impressed with the guys that he offered 1D a recording contract with his record label, Syco Records. After a four-month *X Factor* tour, One Direction went straight into the recording studio to create their first album.

Recording an album was everything the boys had dreamed of! "We got lots of say in the album, actually," Liam told irishtimes.com. "We got to choose a lot of the songs and that sort of stuff." The guys even helped with some of the songwriting!

One Direction's first single, "What Makes You Beautiful," was released on 11th September, 2011, and it immediately shot to number one on the UK Singles Chart. 1D followed it up with their second single, "Gotta Be You," on 11th November, 2011, and their debut album, *Up All Night*, released a week later on 18th November, 2011. It was an instant hit – reaching number two on the UK charts and making the top ten in eighteen other countries.

The guys won the 2011 4Music Awards for "Best Group", "Best Breakthrough", and "Best Video", and also won the 2012 Brit Award for "Best British Single" for "What Makes You Beautiful", beating Adele. They also went on tour all over the country, with most shows selling out within minutes.

Next up, One Direction crossed the pond to take on America. The band made history on 13th March, 2012, when they released *Up All Night* at number one on the American charts. They were the first British group to ever have a number one debut in the US. Harry told cbsnews.com, "It's beyond a dream come true for us."

1. All of the One Direction band members are from England except:

   ☐ A. Harry   ☐ B. Liam   ☐ C. Louis   ☑ D. Niall

2. One Direction became a band on this reality TV show:

   ☐ A. *Pop Idol*   ☑ B. *The X Factor*
   ☐ C. *Britain's Got Talent* ☐ D. *The Voice*

3. In the reality TV competition where One Direction got their start, 1D came in:

   ☐ A. First place   ☑ B. Third place   ☐ C. Fifth place   ☐ D. Last place

4. This 1D member thought up the name One Direction:

   ☐ A. Liam   ☐ B. Zayn   ☑ C. Harry   ☐ D. Niall

5. The boys of One Direction work with this toy brand:

   ☑ A. Pokémon   ☐ B. Bakugan
   ☐ C. Yo Gabba Gabba   ☐ D. Scooby-Doo

6. 1D's official Twitter handle is:

   ☐ A. @1D4Ever   ☑ B. @onedirection
   ☐ C. @1Direction   ☐ D. @1DMusic

7. Which of these singers is not in One Direction?

   ☐ A. Harry Styles   ☐ B. Liam Payne
   ☐ C. Louis Tomlinson   ☑ D. Matt Cardle

8. The One Direction music video for "Gotta Be You" includes a Volkswagen Beetle in what colour?

   ☑ A. Baby blue   ☐ B. Bright red
   ☐ C. Lemon yellow   ☐ D. Light green

9. One Direction's music video for "One Thing" features the band riding around London in a:

- ☐ A. Volkswagen Beetle
- ☑ C. Red double-decker bus
- ☐ B. Chevy pickup truck
- ☐ D. Mercedes convertible

10. One Direction's first official single was:

- ☑ A. "What Makes You Beautiful"
- ☐ C. "One Thing"
- ☐ B. "Gotta Be You"
- ☐ D. "More Than This"

11. 1D set what record in the US?

- ☐ A. First boy band to have a number one debut in the US
- ☐ B. Youngest boy band to have a number one debut in the US
- ☑ C. First British group to have a number one debut in the US
- ☐ D. Cutest boy band to have a number one debut in the US

12. The music video for "What Makes You Beautiful" was filmed where?

- ☐ A. In a forest
- ☑ C. On a beach
- ☐ B. At a shopping centre
- ☐ D. In an aeroplane

13. 1D is often compared to this 1960s British band:

- ☑ A. The Beatles
- ☐ C. Herman's Hermits
- ☐ B. The Rolling Stones
- ☐ D. The Kinks

14. The boys of One Direction beat Adele to win this 2012 Brit Award:

- ☐ A. Best Breakthrough Artist
- ☐ C. Best Music Video
- ☐ B. Best Group
- ☑ D. Best British Single

15. This TV judge signed 1D to their first record deal:

- ☑ A. Simon Cowell
- ☐ C. Kylie Minogue
- ☐ B. Nicole Scherzinger
- ☐ D. Usher

All About Harry

arry Edward Styles was born on 1ˢᵗ February, 1994, in Evesham, England, to proud parents Anne and Des. Harry loved singing as a child – especially Elvis Presley's songs. Harry's parents got a divorce when he was seven, but he and his older sister, Gemma, have always been close with both their mum and their dad.

The older Harry got, the more important music became to him. Harry became the lead singer for the band White Eskimo with friends Haydn Morris, Nick Clough, and Will Sweeny at Holmes Chapel Comprehensive School. The group practised whenever they could and even landed a few gigs at a wedding and some school events after performing at a Battle of the Bands in their town. Luckily, Harry's former bandmates are now his biggest supporters. Harry gained a lot of confidence while performing with White Eskimo, and his charismatic stage style definitely makes him a superstar with One Direction!

STAR STATS

> **Full Name:** Harry Edward Styles

> **Nickname:** Barry

> **Birthday:** 1st February, 1994

> **Siblings:** older sister, Gemma

> **Home Town:** Holmes Chapel, England

> **Best Friend:** Louis Tomlinson

> **Favourite Film:** *Love Actually*

> **Favourite Bands:** Foster the People, Coldplay, Kings of Leon, The Beatles

> **Favourite TV Show:** *Family Guy*

> **Favourite Colour:** pink

> **Likes:** Laser Quest

> **Dislikes:** roller coasters, olives

> **Twitter Handle:** @Harry_Styles

When _____ had to go on a family holiday the
GIRL'S NAME

same week that One Direction was playing in _____,
NAME OF TOWN
her

home town, she was devastated. _____ couldn't believe
SAME GIRL'S NAME

that she was going to miss seeing _____, her favourite
ONE DIRECTION BAND MEMBER

member of 1D! She tried to make the best of the situation – after

all, she was in _____! She put on her _____ and
HOLIDAY SPOT   HOLIDAY OUTFIT

spent plenty of time _____. Soon her holiday was over
HOLIDAY ACTIVITY

and _____ headed back to _____ with her family.
SAME GIRL'S NAME   SAME NAME OF TOWN

When _____ got off the plane, she noticed a
SAME GIRL'S NAME

commotion in the airport. There were _____ and
PLURAL NOUN

reporters everywhere! They all seemed to be looking for something.

_____ pushed her way _____ through the crowd
SAME GIRL'S NAME   ADVERB

and, to her surprise, saw the _____ guys of One Direction
ADJECTIVE

walking right towards her! They were on their way to catch their

flight to _____ for their next concert.
EXOTIC DESTINATION

    Just then, the crowd pushed forward and _____
SAME GIRL'S NAME

was knocked _____ to the ground. She landed with a
ADVERB

_____ and cried out. _____ saw her fall and
NOISE   ONE DIRECTION BAND MEMBER

hurried over to help her up, followed by the rest of the band. "I'm

so sorry you fell," _____ exclaimed. "Let me help you."
ONE DIRECTION BAND MEMBER

He pulled _____ to her feet and gave her a big hug.
SAME GIRL'S NAME

    "I'm OK," she answered. "Thanks for your help." He gave her

a/an _____ kiss on the cheek and then hurried off with the
ADJECTIVE

rest of 1D. _____ sighed. It was the _____ end to
SAME GIRL'S NAME   ADJECTIVE

a holiday ever!

Liam James Payne was born to parents Karen and Geoff on 29th August, 1993, in Wolverhampton, England. But little Liam had health problems. One of his kidneys wasn't working, so Liam spent most of his childhood in and out of hospitals. Having a great family to support him made all of those doctor's appointments much easier to deal with!

In high school, Liam was one of the stars of his school's cross-country team, and he also took boxing lessons. Liam also had a serious passion for music. He always dreamed of singing, but he was also interested in the business side of the music industry. He studied music technology at the City of Wolverhampton College with plans to look for a behind-the-scenes music job after he graduated. Luckily, Liam never gave up on singing, and auditioned for *The X Factor* twice – once in 2008 and again in 2010, when he landed in One Direction!

STAR STATS

> **Full Name:** Liam James Payne

> **Nickname:** Ian

> **Birthday:** 29th August, 1993

> **Siblings:** two older sisters, Ruth and Nicola

> **Home Town:** Wolverhampton, England

> **Favourite Film:** all 3 *Toy Story* films

> **Favourite Bands:** Two Door Cinema Club, Bing Crosby, John Mayer

> **Favourite Style Product:** his pink hair straighteners

> **Favourite Colour:** blue

> **Known As:** the "Dad" of One Direction

> **Likes:** surprises, aftershave, singing in the shower

> **Dislikes:** flying, spoons

> **Twitter Handle:** @Real_Liam_Payne

1. The cuties of 1D performed this song at the 2012 *Nickelodeon Kids' Choice Awards:*

☑ A. "Up All Night"   ☐ B. "Forever Young"
☐ C. "What Makes You Beautiful"   ☐ D. "One Thing"

2. Liam sang this song for his *X Factor* audition:

☐ A. "So Sick"   ☐ B. "Let Me Love You"   ☑ C. "Cry Me a River"
☐ D. "Hey There Delilah"   ☐ E. "Isn't She Lovely"

3. Harry sang this song for his *X Factor* audition:

☐ A. "So Sick"   ☐ B. "Let Me Love You"   ☐ C. "Cry Me a River"
☐ D. "Hey There Delilah"   ☑ E. "Isn't She Lovely"

4. Niall sang this song for his *X Factor* audition:

☑ A. "So Sick"   ☐ B. "Let Me Love You"   ☐ C. "Cry Me a River"
☐ D. "Hey There Delilah"   ☐ E. "Isn't She Lovely"

5. Zayn sang this song for his *X Factor* audition:

☐ A. "So Sick"   ☑ B. "Let Me Love You"   ☐ C. "Cry Me a River"
☐ D. "Hey There Delilah"   ☐ E. "Isn't She Lovely"

6. Louis sang this song for his *X Factor* audition:

☐ A. "So Sick"   ☐ B. "Let Me Love You"   ☐ C. "Cry Me a River"
☑ D. "Hey There Delilah"   ☐ E. "Isn't She Lovely"

7. Which of these songs did One Direction not cover on *The X Factor*?

☐ A. "My Life Would Suck Without You" ☐ B. "Chasing Cars"
☐ C. "Kids in America"   ☑ D. "Firework"

8. This 1D star was nearly cut from *The X Factor* for not wanting to dance at boot camp:

☐ A. Liam   ☐ B. Niall   ☐ C. Harry   ☐ D. Louis   ☑ E. Zayn

9. One Direction's summer 2012 tour took place in which country?
- ☐ A. England
- ☑ C. the United States
- ☐ B. Australia
- ☐ D. Japan

10. 1D's live performance concert DVD is called:
- ☑ A. *Up All Night: The Live Tour*
- ☐ C. *One Direction Live*
- ☐ B. *Forever Young: 1D Live*
- ☐ D. *A Day with 1D Live*

11. Which fellow *X Factor* contestant is opening for One Direction on their summer 2012 tour?
- ☐ A. Rebecca Ferguson
- ☑ C. Olly Murs
- ☐ B. Matt Cardle
- ☐ D. JLS

12. What song did 1D record to release if they won *The X Factor*?
- ☐ A. "Up All Night"
- ☐ C. "What Makes You Beautiful"
- ☑ B. "Forever Young"
- ☐ D. "Gotta Be You"

13. 1D starred as the musical guest on this comedy show:
- ☑ A. *Saturday Night Live*
- ☐ C. *So Random!*
- ☐ B. *Punk'd*
- ☐ D. *Off Their Rockers*

14. 1D guest starred and performed on this Nickelodeon TV show:
- ☑ A. *iCarly*
- ☐ C. *Supah Ninjas*
- ☐ B. *Victorious*
- ☐ D. *Fred: The Show*

15. 1D went on tour with this Nickelodeon TV and music star:
- ☐ A. Miranda Cosgrove
- ☑ C. Big Time Rush
- ☐ B. Victoria Justice
- ☐ D. How to Rock

All About Zayn

The brown-eyed cutie known as Zayn was born Zain Javadd Malik on 12th January, 1993. Zayn is half-Pakistani, by his dad, Yaser, and half-English, from his mum, Tricia. Zayn grew up near Bradford, in England. He and his three sisters got picked on a lot when they were younger because of their mixed heritage. It didn't help that they moved several times and the Malik kids had to change schools.

But Zayn really came into his own when he began school at Tong High School, where he excelled at performing arts. Zayn turned into a charming, charismatic star when he hit the stage. He starred in several of Tong High's musicals, including *Grease*. *The X Factor* took Zayn's love of performing to a new level but he was able to step up to the challenge thanks to his friends and family cheering him on at home!

STAR STATS

> Full Name: **Zain Javadd Malik**

> Nickname: **Wayne, Zayn**

> Birthday: **12th January, 1993**

> Siblings: **sisters Doniya, Waliyha, and Safaa**

> Home Town: **Bradford, England**

> Favourite Film: ***Scarface***

> Favourite Bands: **Usher, Robin Thicke, Michael Jackson, Ne-Yo**

> Favourite Colour: **red**

> Bad Habit: **checks himself in every mirror he sees**

> Likes: **scary films, dancing**

> Dislikes: **crust on sandwiches, swimming**

> Tattoos: **Zayn's grandfather's name in Arabic, a yin yang symbol, the Japanese symbols for "born lucky," and crossed fingers**

> Twitter Handle: **@zaynmalik**

1. *Scarface* is which 1D band member's favourite film?

   ❏ **A.** Liam   ❏ **B.** Niall   ❏ **C.** Harry   ❏ **D.** Louis   ☑ **E.** Zayn

2. Michael Bublé is which 1D band member's favourite singer?

   ❏ **A.** Liam   ☑ **B.** Niall   ❏ **C.** Harry   ❏ **D.** Louis   ❏ **E.** Zayn

3. *Grease* is the favourite film of which two 1D band members?

   ❏ A. Liam and Harry   ☑ B. Niall and Louis
   ❏ C. Harry and Louis   ❏ D. Louis and Zayn

4. Which 1D band member's favourite TV show is *Family Guy*?

   ❏ **A.** Liam   ❏ **B.** Niall   ☑ **C.** Harry   ❏ **D.** Louis   ❏ **E.** Zayn

5. What is Louis's favourite vegetable?

   ☑ A. Carrots   ❏ B. Broccoli
   ❏ C. Celery   ❏ D. Cauliflower

6. Which 1D band member's favourite activity is sunbathing?

   ❏ **A.** Liam   ❏ **B.** Niall   ❏ **C.** Harry   ☑ **D.** Louis   ❏ **E.** Zayn

7. Which 1D band member might you run into playing laser tag?

   ❏ **A.** Liam   ❏ **B.** Niall   ☑ **C.** Harry   ❏ **D.** Louis   ❏ **E.** Zayn

8. Which 1D band member is considered the favourite with female fans?

   ❏ **A.** Liam   ❏ **B.** Niall   ☑ **C.** Harry   ❏ **D.** Louis   ❏ **E.** Zayn

9. Which 1D band member hates olives?

   ❏ **A.** Liam   ❏ **B.** Niall   ☑ **C.** Harry   ❏ **D.** Louis   ❏ **E.** Zayn

10. Which 1D band member hates mayonnaise?

☐ **A.** Liam ☑ **B.** Niall ☐ **C.** Harry ☐ **D.** Louis ☐ **E.** Zayn

11. Which 1D band member can't swim?

☐ **A.** Liam ☐ **B.** Niall ☐ **C.** Harry ☐ **D.** Louis ☑ **E.** Zayn

12. Which 1D band member's favourite colour is pink?

☐ **A.** Liam ☐ **B.** Niall ☑ **C.** Harry ☐ **D.** Louis ☐ **E.** Zayn

13. Purple is the favourite colour of which 1D band member?

☐ **A.** Liam ☐ **B.** Niall ☐ **C.** Harry ☑ **D.** Louis ☐ **E.** Zayn

14. Which 1D band member loves surprises?

☑ **A.** Liam ☐ **B.** Niall ☐ **C.** Harry ☐ **D.** Louis ☐ **E.** Zayn

15. Which 1D band member has a reputation as a practical joker?

☐ **A.** Liam ☐ **B.** Niall ☐ **C.** Harry ☑ **D.** Louis ☐ **E.** Zayn

Louis William Tomlinson was born on 24th December, 1991, in Doncaster, England, to proud parents Johanna and Mark Tomlinson. Louis was joined a few years later by younger sisters Charlotte, Félicité, and then twins, Daisy and Phoebe.

Louis wasn't the first star in the family. As babies, his twin sisters landed a role on *Fat Friends*, a popular TV programme, and Louis got to appear as an extra on the show, too! He also appeared in *If I Had You*, a feature-length drama, and on another TV programme, *Waterloo Road*. Louis loved acting and singing, but school was also important to him.

At Hall Cross School, Louis worked hard in his lessons and found plenty of time to star in the school's plays and musicals. Louis had never been shy about his dream of being a professional performer, so when he auditioned for *The X Factor* and joined One Direction, no one was surprised!

STAR STATS

- > Full Name: **Louis William Tomlinson**
- > Nickname: **Hughy**
- > Birthday: **24th December, 1991**
- > Siblings: **sisters Charlotte, Félicité, Daisy, and Phoebe**
- > Home Town: **Doncaster, England**
- > Best Friend: **Harry Styles**
- > Favourite Film: *Grease*

- > Favourite Bands: **Bombay Bicycle Club, The Fray**
- > Favourite Vegetable: **carrots**
- > Favourite Colour: **purple**
- > Likes: **sunbathing, silly voices, practical jokes**
- > Dislikes: **not being able to Tweet on planes, being pale**
- > Twitter Handle: **@Louis_Tomlinson**

Niall James Horan was born on 13th September, 1993, in Ireland. He and his older brother, Greg, were inseparable growing up. Unfortunately, Niall's parents, Maura and Bobby, split up when Niall was five, but they have both always been very supportive of his dreams.

Niall surprised everyone when he started singing out loud in the car one day and his dad and aunt thought the radio was on! It was clear Niall had some serious musical talent, so his family got him a guitar when he was old enough to learn to play.

Niall attended high school at Coláiste Mhuire. He sang and played guitar in a few local concerts and always wowed the crowds. Still, Niall knew that his *X Factor* audition competing against 10,000 other people in his town was the biggest audition of his life! Luckily, Niall never doubted his talent or his dreams – he's now a member of One Direction!

> Full Name: **Niall James Horan**

> Nickname: **Kyle**

> Birthday: **13th September, 1993**

> Siblings: **older brother, Greg**

> Home Town: **Mullingar, Ireland**

> Favourite Film: *Grease*

> Favourite Bands: **The Script, Ed Sheeran, Bon Jovi**

> Favourite Singer: **Michael Bublé**

> Favourite Colour: **yellow**

> Likes: **football**

> Dislikes: **mayonnaise, clowns**

> Twitter Handle: **@NiallOfficial**

1. What is Harry's middle name?

   ❏ A. Javadd ❏ B. James ☑ C. Edward ❏ D. William

2. What colour are Liam's eyes?

   ☑ A. Brown ❏ B. Blue ❏ C. Green ❏ D. Hazel

3. Who is the only blond in 1D?

   ❏ A. Liam ☑ B. Niall ❏ C. Harry ❏ D. Louis ❏ E. Zayn

4. Which 1D band member's home town is Mullingar, Ireland?

   ❏ A. Liam ☑ B. Niall ❏ C. Harry ❏ D. Louis ❏ E. Zayn

5. Which 1D band member can't stop checking himself out in mirrors?

   ☑ A. Liam ❏ B. Niall ❏ C. Harry ❏ D. Louis ❏ E. Zayn

6. Which 1D band member can't live without his pink hair straighteners?

   ☑ A. Liam ❏ B. Niall ❏ C. Harry ☑ D. Louis ❏ E. Zayn

7. Which 1D band member has told the rest of the band that they can't date his little sisters?

   ❏ A. Liam ❏ B. Niall ❏ C. Harry ☑ D. Louis ❏ E. Zayn

8. Which 1D band member has four tattoos?

   ❏ A. Liam ❏ B. Niall ❏ C. Harry ❏ D. Louis ☑ E. Zayn

9. Which 1D band member is nicknamed Hughy?

   ❏ A. Liam ❏ B. Niall ❏ C. Harry ☑ D. Louis ❏ E. Zayn

10. What is Niall's nickname in the band?

    ☑ A. Kyle ❏ B. Miles ❏ C. Ni-Ni ❏ D. Ireland

11. Which band member was in the band White Eskimo before joining 1D?

   ❏ **A. Liam**   ❏ **B. Niall**   ☑ **C. Harry**   ❏ **D. Louis**   ❏ **E. Zayn**

12. Liam only has one functioning:

   ☑ **A. Kidney**   ❏ **B. Lung**   ❏ **C. Big toe**   ❏ **D. Ear**

13. Who is the shortest member of 1D?

   ❏ **A. Liam**   ❏ **B. Niall**   ❏ **C. Harry**   ❏ **D. Louis**   ☑ **E. Zayn**

14. This 1D cutie used to take boxing lessons:

   ☑ **A. Liam**   ❏ **B. Niall**   ❏ **C. Harry**   ❏ **D. Louis**   ❏ **E. Zayn**

15. Louis appeared on this TV show as a child:

   ❏ **A. _The Teletubbies_**   ☑ **B. _Fat Friends_**
   ❏ **C. _Britain's Got Talent_**   ❏ **D. _In the Night Garden_**

Stylin' with 1D

The guys of One Direction have made a splash with their good looks, smooth dance moves, and catchy music, but they've also made a big impact when it comes to fashion. Liam, Harry, Zayn, Louis, and Niall have made preppy-cool super chic.

All of the guys love wearing dark jeans, polo shirts, button-down shirts, blazers, and scarves. Of course, each band member makes his own unique style statement as well. Zayn generally chooses baggier pants, snowy white trainers, and knitted hats. Niall loves buttoned-up polo shirts, Henleys, and hoodies, but his blond locks are his signature look! Harry rocks plain T-shirts with cozy sweaters or fashionable blazers, all of which look cute with his tousled curls. Liam is definitely the most low-key member of the group when it comes to fashion. He usually chooses checked button-down shirts paired with worn-in jeans. Louis is easily the most fashionable member of 1D. He mixes and matches jeans, khakis, and brightly coloured pants with sharp blazers, cardigans, and suspenders.

When it comes to awards shows, the guys go all out in modern-cut suits, crisp shirts, and skinny ties – making sure they look irresistible on the red carpet! For performances, the guys go for a co-ordinated look. They usually sport a mix of blazers, cardigans, sports jackets, button-down shirts, and jeans or chinos. They almost always choose brighter colours when performing to ensure that even their fans in the back row can see them! Of course, for downtime, you can find the guys wearing jeans, T-shirts, and hoodies just like any other normal teenage boys. No matter where you spot the guys of 1D, you can be sure that they will always look stylish!

Quiz #5: Famous Friends

1. 1D has a friendly rivalry with this British boy band:

   ☐ A. JLS
   ☑ C. McFly
   ☑ B. The Wanted
   ☐ D. Boyzone

2. This teen pop sensation hung out with 1D in the studio and is in talks to collaborate with the band:

   ☐ A. Joe Jonas
   ☑ C. Justin Bieber
   ☐ B. Cody Simpson
   ☐ D. Nick Jonas

3. The 1D guys met this Nick star when they guest starred on her show:

   ☑ A. Miranda Cosgrove
   ☐ C. Keke Palmer
   ☐ B. Victoria Justice
   ☐ D. Nathalia Ramos

4. This country and pop star is rumoured to have a crush on Harry:

   ☐ A. Carrie Underwood
   ☐ C. Jennette McCurdy
   ☐ B. Kellie Pickler
   ☑ D. Taylor Swift

5. Harry couldn't wait to meet this pop star after she told reporters she thought he was a star:

   ☐ A. Beyoncé
   ☑ C. Rihanna
   ☐ B. Miley Cyrus
   ☐ D. Katy Perry

6. Zayn dated this fellow *X Factor* contestant:

   ☐ A. Cher Lloyd
   ☐ C. Pippa Middleton
   ☑ B. Rebecca Ferguson
   ☐ D. Alexandra Burke

7. 1D met this funny Latina when she hosted *SNL* with them:

   ☑ A. Sofia Vergara
   ☐ C. Salma Hayek
   ☐ B. Penelope Cruz
   ☐ D. Selena Gomez

8. This *X Factor* judge and Australian pop princess is still friendly with the 1D boys:

   ❑ A. Dannii Minogue   ☑ B. Kylie Minogue

   ❑ C. Nicole Scherzinger ❑ D. Britney Spears

9. This British rocker's daughter interviewed the guys on the 2012 *Nickelodeon Kids' Choice Awards* orange carpet:

   ❑ A. Peaches Geldof   ❑ B. Lily Collins

   ☑ C. Kelly Osbourne   ❑ D. Pippa Middleton

10. The high-school singers on this TV show cover "What Makes You Beautiful" on an episode:

   ❑ A. *Jessie*   ❑ B. *A.N.T. Farm*

   ❑ C. *Victorious*   ☑ D. *Glee*

Mall Mania: A Fill-in-the-Blanks Story

When the guys of One Direction arrived in _____,

<small>YOUR TOWN</small>

they were really _____ to meet their fans at the local

<small>EMOTION</small>

shopping centre. They had a/an _____ surprise set up for

<small>ADJECTIVE</small>

one of their fans, and they couldn't wait to meet her.

All of the fans visiting the mall put their names into a

_____ when they arrived. Then before the autograph

<small>NOUN</small>

signing began, _____ pulled one name out. He announced

<small>1D BAND MEMBER</small>

the winner – it was _____ – and invited her to come

<small>YOUR NAME</small>

backstage to have _____ with the band.

<small>FOOD</small>

When _____ walked into the backstage room,

<small>YOUR NAME</small>

the guys were thrilled. _____ was _____!

<small>YOUR NAME</small>   <small>ADJECTIVE</small>

She had a cool _____ on and looked so _____

<small>ARTICLE OF CLOTHING</small>   <small>ADJECTIVE</small>

wearing _____ lipstick. They all sat down to have some

<small>COLOUR</small>

_____ and _____, and asked _____
   FOOD   DRINK   YOUR NAME

all about herself. She told them that she loves _____ and
                                                 YOUR FAVOURITE HOBBY

_____, and that she wants to be a _____ when
 YOUR FAVOURITE SUBJECT   PROFESSION

she grows up.

   The boys all thought _____ was _____,
                          YOUR NAME   ADJECTIVE

but _____ especially liked her. He gave _____
    YOUR FAVOURITE 1D BAND MEMBER   YOUR NAME

a special gift – a _____ necklace in the shape of a
                    GEMSTONE

_____. _____ loved it! She gave Liam, Harry,
 SHAPE   YOUR NAME

Zayn, Niall, and Louis all big hugs, and thanked them for the

_____ surprise. The guys all promised to call her the next
 ADJECTIVE

time they were in _____. They were so glad the fan that
                   YOUR TOWN

won had been so _____. It was an awesome trip to the
                 ADJECTIVE

_____ shopping centre!
 YOUR TOWN

Quiz #6: Which 1D Cutie Is Right for You?

1. Your ideal first date would be:

   ❑ A. A cinema date   ❑ B. A trip to the arcade   ❑ C. A nice meal out
   ❑ D. Tickets to a comedy show   ☑ E. A total surprise from start to finish

2. You always go for guys with:

   ❑ A. A great smile   ❑ B. Curls   ❑ C. Straight, shaggy hair
   ❑ D. Deep brown eyes   ☑ E. Blond hair

3. Your favourite food to share with a date is:

   ❑ A. Fried chicken   ❑ B. Tacos   ❑ C. Pizza
   ❑ D. Dessert   ☑ E. Chinese food

4. You can't resist:

   ❑ A. A short cutie   ❑ B. A fashionable guy   ❑ C. A star actor
   ❑ D. An athletic guy   ☑ E. A guy who plays guitar

5. You love a guy who rocks:

   ❑ A. Pure white trainers   ❑ B. A blazer   ❑ C. Suspenders
   ❑ D. Checked shirts   ☑ E. Polo shirts

6. If your date played a practical joke on you, you would:

   ❑ A. Laugh! He didn't do it in public, so it's all good.
   ❑ B. Plot a joke to play on him with his best friend.
   ❑ C. Play one on him to get even.
   ❑ D. Let him buy you dinner to make up for it.
   ☑ E. Admit he got you good - you aren't the type to get even.

7. You can't imagine a better way to be asked out than if your crush:

   ❏ A. Challenged you to a dance-off, with the winner picking the activity.
   ❏ B. Winked at you and asked for your number.
   ❏ C. Tweeted you.
   ❏ D. Sang you a song.
   ☑ E. Told you that you were the most beautiful girl he'd ever seen.

8. You would most want to dance with your crush to which song?

   ❏ A. Michael Jackson's "Thriller"
   ❏ B. Coldplay's "Paradise"
   ❏ C. The Fray's "How to Save a Life"
   ❏ D. Bing Crosby's "Waltzing in a Dream"
   ☑ E. Bon Jovi's "Livin' on a Prayer"

9. If your crush took you to a film, you would pick:

   ❏ A. A scary film   ❏ B. A romantic comedy   ❏ C. A comedy
   ❏ D. An animated flick   ☑ E. A musical

10. Your perfect cinema snack to share with your crush would be:

   ❏ A. Chicken nuggets   ☑ B. Popcorn   ❏ C. Cookie dough
   ❏ D. Chocolate   ❏ E. Spring rolls

11. If your crush invited you over for dinner with his family, you'd look forward to:

   ❏ A. Trying out authentic Pakistani food.
   ❏ B. Meeting his former bandmates over dessert.
   ❏ C. Meeting his little sisters.
   ❏ D. A dinner that required no spoons.
   ☑ E. A dish made from real Irish potatoes. ✓

12. Which sporty activity would you like to do with your crush?

   ❏ A. Basketball   ❏ B. Tennis   ❏ C. Surfing   ❏ D. Running   ☑ E. Football

13. Your favourite 1D singer is:

☐ **A. Zayn**   ☐ **B. Harry**   ☐ **C. Louis**   ☐ **D. Liam**   ☑ **E. Niall**

14. If your date brought you your favourite flowers, they would be:

☐ **A. Red roses**   ☐ **B. Pink peonies**   ☐ **C. Purple irises**
☐ **D. Blue hydrangeas**   ☑ **E. Yellow tulips**

All the Answers

Check your answers from all of the quizzes and see just how big a 1D fan you are!

Quiz #1: 1.D 2.B 3.B 4.C 5.A 6.B 7.D 8.A 9.C 10.A 11.C 12.C 13.A 14.D 15.A

Quiz #2: 1.C 2.C 3.E 4.A 5.B 6.D 7.D 8.E 9.C 10.A 11.C 12.B 13.A 14.A 15.C

Quiz #3: 1.E 2.B 3.B 4.C 5.A 6.D 7.C 8.C 9.C 10.B 11.E 12.C 13.D 14.A 15.D

Quiz #4: 1.C 2.A 3.B 4.B 5.E 6.A 7.D 8.E 9.D 10.A 11.C 12.A 13.E 14.A 15.B

Quiz #5: 1.B 2.C 3.A 4.D 5.C 6.B 7.A 8.B 9.C 10.D

Quiz #6: If you answered mostly As, then your 1D match is Zayn. If you answered mostly Bs, then your 1D match is Harry. If you answered mostly Cs, then your 1D match is Louis. If you answered mostly Ds, then your 1D match is Liam. If you answered mostly Es, then your 1D match is Niall.

If you answered most of the questions right, you are a 1D SUPERFAN! You follow the band's Tweets, read every interview the boys give, have seen all of their official music videos, and never miss a TV appearance. If you ever get the chance to meet 1D, the guys will definitely be impressed with your dedication!

If you answered half of the questions right, you are a pretty big 1D fan. You love One Direction's music and you know all the basics. If you ever meet the band, you'll have plenty to talk to the guys about!

If you didn't get many questions right, you may need to brush up on your One Direction facts. After all, you wouldn't want to be unprepared in case you get to meet the 1D cuties in person some day!